Soulful thoughts.

For it wasn't into my ear you whispered,

but into my soul.

Printed in Victoria, Canada

National Library of Canada Cataloguing in Publication

Williams, Jennifer C
Soulful thoughts : for it wasn't into my ear you whispered but into my soul / Jennifer C.
Williams.
ISBN 1-4120-1019-5
I. Title.
PS8595.I444S68 2003   C811'.6   C2003-904325-8

TRAFFORD

This book was published *on-demand* in cooperation with Trafford Publishing. On-demand
publishing is a unique process and service of making a book available for retail sale to the public
taking advantage of on-demand manufacturing and Internet marketing. **On-demand publishing**
includes promotions, retail sales, manufacturing, order fulfilment, accounting and collecting royalties
on behalf of the author.

Suite 6E, 2333 Government St., Victoria, B.C. V8T 4P4, CANADA

Phone	250-383-6864	Toll-free	1-888-232-4444 (Canada & US)
Fax	250-383-6804	E-mail	sales@trafford.com
Web site	www.trafford.com	TRAFFORD PUBLISHING IS A DIVISION OF TRAFFORD HOLDINGS LTD.	
Trafford Catalogue #03-1388		www.trafford.com/robots/03-1388.html	

10   9   8   7   6   5   4   3   2   1

Introduction.

I've been writing poetry since the age 14yrs and I have kept myself a journal from the age 11yrs; but I never thought for one minute that I would be collecting my words of experiences into a book. These words were just a way for me to get through life, a way of expressing my innermost feelings. Most of my poetry is about love, relationships and teen life situations – seeing that I'm only in my early 20's.

The reason I decided to write this book and publish it was cause of an inspiration of a song artist who wrote a book herself and made me see this is something I can share. Artist, Ashanti in her book "FOOLISH/UNFOOLISH Reflections on Love." – helped me to realize the way I was feeling, I wasn't alone. She may not know me, but cause of her inspiration I'm grateful. Now with the rest of the world I can share my most

inner thoughts and hope to inspire others the same.

Opening Your Eyes.

This is a poetry book of the mind.

A book where I can open my eyes to any and everything...

Opening my eyes to things I only can see.

Opening my eyes to open my heart.

Knowing the words written in this book...

Is all about life experiences.

All about my life changes

Happy moments

Sad moments

Vex moments

And of course the moments that aren't explainable.

Hurt and sorrows

Pain with tears.

But...

There are always happy moments as well.

When being touch is a wonderful feeling.

Being kissed

Being hugged

Making love

Having someone who truly cares for you.

Life is all about opening your eyes.

LIFE

Remember the day when things were ever so
simple, when life was ever so sweet. The journey
of a thousand miles begins with the first step.

Isn't, As It Seems.

Learn that life isn't always

what it seem to be.

Time and time again you run,

run away from something you're not

even sure about.

The unknown world that's

where you are.

Life is so unknown that time is short,

too many decisions to make.

Times are wasted.

Your heart skips beats, cause too much

heart-full decisions.

Use & Abuse.

Life is use and abuse

That's all we have now is destruction....

Don't we all wish for the sunshine...no more

rain in the clouds

We all want to cry out

No hiding places for tears.

No matter how much we try to put our pain

to the back of our life's.

Survive = Suffering.

To live is to survive, to survive is to suffer.

One man can change the world but only with

our father totally at heart.

Otherwise it's just another brother dead.

A man with too much pain and argue

could never really have our father at heart.

And

changes of this man would start happening

without him even realizing it.

Hurting the closest ones to him without knowing it.

You never realize change unless you have

prepared for it.

There are times when you wonder if life is everything you

expected.

What do you really expect? That's the question.

So many questions and so few answers, but

who's the one to answer the question for us?

Life! Has so many questions but the unfair thing is

that we all have to find out all by our self.

Life is love, respect, peace and harmony.

The question is what is really love?

What is really respect?

What is really peace?

What is really harmony?

Does anybody honestly really know the meaning of these

words?

If you don't know the meaning of these words, then what is

life?

I bet you don't know.

Who's the one to know the way one feels, who's the one to

give advice?

Why is it so hard to understand this big world, why can'

someone just tell me.

You're stuck in the clouds and you just don't know how to

get out.

You yell HELP!!!

No one hears.

Do You Remember.

Do you remember when you were a baby and you had not

a thing in this world to care for?

Do you remember how you would cry if things didn't go your

way?

Do you remember the smile that would be on your face

when your

mother picked you up from daycare?

Now you look back on these days and wish that you could

turn things back...

bills and more bills to pay.

Working and doing school because you have so much future

plans.

Your new life is in front of you now and for some reason you

wish you could turn

back to when you were young again.

So much responsibilities that now you want to walk

backwards and pray to fall

back in time when life was easy.

Why?

What is this world all really about?

There are times in my life that all I want to do

is laid back and cry.

But ...

What is that truly going to do for me?

Too many questions and I just cannot seem

to find the answer.

Why? Why? Why?

Please tell me why I cannot find the answers

to my questions.

Close Your Eyes Once.

Life may seem the most wonderful

until that day.

The minute you close your eyes things changes.

What are you to do now?

Maybe close your eyes again hoping that it would

turn back to the way it was.

Tears and heartaches, trying to find out

what to do next.

Close your eyes once...

It changes everything.

Extent Of Life

Have you ever wonder how far people would go

for something they want.

Have you ever wonder why people dare you,

cause...they may actually want you to do it.

Do you believe that this person would actually

stay to end of the dare.

So cause of a question like that you take the chance to

see...

To see what extent life going to bring.

Born To.

So many times I've changed my mind

I guess I was born to make mistakes

But...

I ain't scared to take the weight

But...

I'm cleva in everything that I do

so mistakes are like.

Diamonds & gems.

Slowly –surely I walk in a natural way

hoping for some eye contact.

To the highest respect...

Slowly - surely I open my heart

to new and old options to

better a relationship.

Slowly – surely I open my eyes to the

beautiful things in life.

Slowly – surely I open my mind to the

comfortable things life can bring

my way.

Slowly – surely I open my door to the

finer things in life.

Slowly – surely greater things are coming.

Greater things of the unknown.

Life Goes On.

Human beings by nature want less suffering and more

happiness.

Reality sadly to say, includes suffering.

The feelings we would fail to acknowledge,

will return to haunt us.

We as humans fluctuate between acceptance and denial,

belief and disbelief, hope and despair.

Confronting people rarely bring the relief we seek.

Confrontation would in many cases actually increases the

pain and prolongs our grief.

In order to say goodbye to someone/thing,

first we need to understand what happened to us

and how we feel about it.

I don't know or understand what happened.

Someone please tell me.

Open Doors & Closed Doors.

Life is about taking chances.

All chances for the better but at times it doesn't

always end up the way you wanted it.

Then that chance has now became a lesson.

One you carry with you!

Doors are always going to open and close.

Be ready!

And when you open that one door do everything

you can to keep it open.

Night Mind Traveler.

You lie in bed...

Thinking about the day.

What did you do with your life today?

What does the future have in store for me?

How long is it going to take to get where I'm going?

Lots of questions...

Traveling the mind...

Which will all be answered one way or another.

So all you do is process and wait!

But...

Your mind travels, further and further.

The Opening Of Doors.

Now it's over.

Now your heart and mind just don't know what to do

anymore.

You say you have nothing left...

Are you saying life is over?

You truly believe that you have lived your life to the fullest.

Do you have unfilled dreams still?

Cause...

Then you still have opening doors.

One door closes and many more opens.

It's up to you...

Life is never over...

Till the day you die.

Even then you live forever.

It's now beginning.

LOVE

Just cause you can't explain it doesn't mean it isn't love. One the magic # no jacket, no umbrella...just warmth he loves me.

Joy / Sorrow.

When you feel like this one person in your life has done

everything you can think of that's when your wonder if it's

LOVE.

You close your eyes and dream for so much but when it

doesn't happen you think to yourself is this really loves I

feel.

In this big wide world is there anything that's possible?

Questions! Because when you really and truly love

someone you would never be able to let go.

The smile on your face when he walks into the room.

The flames that burns within when you touch

you run so fast but don't get anywhere.

You call so loud but no one hears.

The pain that burns inside, how do you heal it.

It's like you're a baby trying to walk, trying to talk but still

nothing happens.

When you cry and you don't understand why... is it

tears of

joy or sorrow.

When You Love.

How do you know when you love

someone?

How do you know it is real?

And when you finally find out that

you found love.

What is the hope that it is going to last!

Love is comfort & caring towards your partner.

Love is so much to me.

When you are describing the one you love

and you can't find such wonderful words towards him

then you know that is LOVE !!

The crazy thing is when you love someone and

you always tell him you love and

one day you just can't say it no more.

Then you wonder is it because you love him so much

that it's now harder to say

or is it because your love is going away?

That's my question!!

The Reasons For Love.

Love and the reasons for love.

People never know what real love is.

They turn in so many different direction hoping that

someone would be able to tell

them.

All they hear is the words of silent.

Nobody know how to explain this wonderful feeling

of LOVE.

Maybe it is not for real,

maybe it is all a joke.

Love is for real and I believe in it

I believe that I am in love.

Love is a kind of passion that is really hard to find.

The one thing is when you do find this love you would for

sure know it is there.

There maybe times when it may not last but you have

to let go and start all over again.

Not let your life always end in sorrow.

Happiness & joy is a wonderful thing so hold on when

you got love!!

Right Man.

It's a dream when you find the right man

The man that understand you.

The man that knows when something is wrong and

when something is extremely right.

This man is the type for man that is there for you even when

you feel like

you need to be alone.

A man who hold your world in his hands.

Comfort, respect, love, peace and cherish able moments

for always.

Love.

Sometimes it's hard for others to realize

the different types of love,

there isn't one

way to love a person nor is there one way

to show a person you love them.

In my eye's every little thing counts and that's

where true love lies.

Share.

The love you share with a love one

Is a wonderful feeling...

When that love one gives you just the

love you need.

The feeling of rushes with the kisses of love.

The feeling of sexually action of making love

and not just sex.

Love is a wonderful feeling.

To stop loving should be a sin.

Love & Happiness.

Love and happiness is the greatest thing

that life can bring.

Finding love isn't easy, it may just be

the hardest thing in life but it's the

best feeling when found.

Loving someone is the

most beautiful thing.

But...

Loving someone and knowing

that this person loves

you back is even more beautiful.

But...

Knowing this person is your

husband to be... is something

more beautiful than

beautiful.

I Want.

I want my baby to think of me

I want my baby to think of me when his hope is gone

I want you to see your life through me

I want to be the reason you get through your day

I want to be the one you turn to when there's pain

Hope's and dreams with me can become reality

Let me be the reason you get through the day

Think of me.

You Know.

Even if I wake up and find the whole world destroy

And god says it's time to go

I'll be happy going.

Knowing that I loved you

And I let you know

Before I go

You have to know the joy you brought to

my life.

As It's Known

As one man has told me...

You can't help whom you fall in love with.

Love control itself in some sense.

Sometimes you have so much to say about how you feel

but it's just not the right place or time

for these words of thoughts.

Loving a man is a wonderful feeling not having him is

the most painful feeling.

So you fight...fight to have.

Love

Just cause you cannot explain it doesn't mean it isn't.

Love isn't always as it seems...

Love is a whole different level of understanding.

Love isn't a real feeling.

Love is a level of trust and understanding.

Two people who can always come to a common ground.

Love is something that no human being would ever

be able to fully define.

Sometimes love is letting go can you understand that?

Maybe not...but I have experience lower and higher

heights of love.

Not saying I know it all but I know just cause

you can't explain it, doesn't mean it

isn't love.

Falling Short.

Have you ever had a love that nothing can explain it...

Falling short!

Words that just never end cause the love is every word

in the books even written.

The only thing that seems to explain this love

is the soulful of the heart.

It's so warm when you think of this love.

To truly explain this love...

This even falls short.

I close my eyes and ask why can't I find

the right words to explain.

Never once was I totally speechless about love.

A love of unexplainable...

Can you tell me.

Dreams.

Close your eyes.

What is the one thing you feel most...

Feeling the power of words not any words but...

Words!

From the soul.

Conversations that goes on within...without even realizing it

Those powerful words

Carries...

You to powerful dreams

Dreams that can make a difference in your life as well as

other

They say follow your heart why not go a step further and

follow your soul.

You have a dream partner...

How do you find your soul mate when you are looking with

your heart.

Your heart will always love even when

you are mad/argue it's cause you love/care.

But your soul... you understand love is just a word.

Being in love is a soul reaction a reaction within.

They say sometimes your mind doesn't do as you tell it to...

more so your soul.

Dreams are real!

FALLING

Someone has your whole world flipping. The person got you feeling like the breeze...easy and free.

Fallin''

One day you just start fallin' and you

don't know where you are heading

then one day when you less expect

it someone's at the other end ready to catch you.

The next question you always seem

to ask yourself, is this the one?

Are you going to spend the rest of

your life with this one?

Time is the only way things are to

be told.

Prays are the way to good.

Maybe this time I wouldn't end

up fallin' again

maybe I have been caught for good

MAYBE!!!.

Emotion To Trust.

Don't tell me trust you....

When it comes to emotions

Emotion is something that can't be control

Just cause things doesn't

work your way...

doesn't mean that 2nd class is going to do any

better

actually you'll only be thinking/ wondering

about how it would be to sit in 1st class

especially when you got a tease of

what that may feel like.

The rush through your body

When being served in all the

right ways.

I Ask For.

What I have is someone

who cares for me

through good times and bad.

He sees me through

He's the sun that brightens up my days

He's friendship, trust, commitment

he's everything

I ask for.

Sexual Feelings.

Have you ever wonder what makes

a man crazy about a woman.

What make a man say your something

different.

Different, how you are now thinking

Thinking of how good you are

and maybe you should just...

Hold back... you know

Sexual feelings are

feelings totally unexplainable

Feel me so I can feel you!

When I Think Of You.

When I think of you

It's like a flame running through my body

heating up emotions

loving ... being held by you

lying with you at nights feels amazing...

even if once

your lips touching mines

your eyes looking into mines

your warm body against mine

your thoughts and care for me is amazing

these are the things that make me love you

love you that you have to be mines

two or none

you are for me.

Mind Travel.

Your mind traveling...

Traveling to higher heights

Heights that you have to be careful

you don't fall.

But if you happen to come just a little close to the edge

make sure someone is there to catch you.

Catch me and keep me.

But there's only one special person that

can keep me.

You Make Me Feel.

When I think of you

my mind just doesn't stop.

It runs from one end of the world to the next

Tenderness ... Romance ...

Gentleman ...

Hold me

Kiss me

Sexually feel me

That's how you make me feel.

Different.

A touch of no control

I just can't hold it

Your cologne, your hands,

Your smile, your intelligence

all a sexually

warmth inside.

You're different and special in every

magical way

Every imaginable way.

Pure & True.

You are so pure and true

We are going to over stand...

I can't imagine why I feel so weak

when he takes my heart in his hands and

kisses it so gently, the way I like it.

I'm in love with him.

So in love.

Speechless.

You are the man that takes words from my mouth

You cause me to be speechless.

Speechless with thoughts of you.

Thoughts that's never ending.

Thoughts of you being my everything.

Everything...

to hold ... kiss and especially

to love.

Express .

Your love, means the world to me.

No words express the joy you bring.

Love from you moves me tenderly

Having you by my side means

the world to me.

You mean the world, galaxy to me.

Love the beyond of

the beyond.

Can't Stop.

I can't stop thinking of you

Can't stop thinking of the way you hold me.

Can't stop thinking of the way you kiss me.

Can't stop thinking of the way you love me.

Can't stop thinking of the way you make love to me.

Can't stop thinking of the way you look at me.

Can't stop thinking of the little things you do that

seem so stupid but so cute at the same time.

I just can't stop thinking of you

even when you make me

mad.

Warmth & Scent.

The warmth of you lying beside me.

The scent of your brown skin.

The warmth of your hand moving up and down

my body.

The scent of your cologne rubbing onto my body.

The warmth of you being inside of me.

The scent of sweet...sexuality when you are

kissing me to non-stop levels.

The warmth of feelings running through my body

when your lips is all over my body.

The scent of magic when you put

you and me together.

In To You.

Every time I'm near you

my whole mood can change from

sour to sweet... in a spilt second.

I truly like what you have done

to me.

I can't even explain the way you

truly make me feel.

It's beyond great.

The dream man of my life...

crazy emotions of heated fire flames within.

I get happy being around you

and

when you're not around I'm the saddest person.

I know you are truly someone

special .

Maybe it's the way you hold me...

Maybe it's the way you talk to me...

Maybe it's the way you kiss me...

I truly like the feeling

when I'm with you.

I'm so in to you!!!

The Truth.

I love him...he's so real, so true

I love him so much that the thought

of him with another woman is something

I truly refuse to accept.

Even if he's on the phone with another woman

friend or not I refuse to accept.

I love him beyond loving a man.

I find myself going through mood changes

when it comes to him.

Any point of time when I don't feel like #ONE.

One man can change your life forever if he's special enough.

A man that gaining him or losing him

is both a scary moment in your life.

Cause...cause...

He's so special.

Freedom.

Everybody wants freedom...

What is freedom?

Can you handle true freedom...

Everybody wants things easy, include me but

sadly I'm telling myself now that things don't come easily.

Especially the best things.

You want freedom...freedom isn't easy.

So why is it call freedom, only cause you can make the

decision.

But...

Your decision is a gamble and a gamble isn't free.

You have to lose one to gain one.

That's what a gamble is!

Freedom = Gamble.

Losing one to gain one isn't freedom.

It's a change.

Better...Worst...

Time shall tell!

Can't help whom you fall in love with.

Heart Beat.

The sun is out...

And your body is warm heated emotions are running wild.

You see that eye catcher from a mile.

Now the regular heartbeat has just speed up.

Butterflies are running wild

over your head, in your stomach.

Cause love...feelings...emotions are all in the air.

The heat beats!

NEVER
LET GO

Hold fast and believe. If you want it to happen all
you got to do is try.

Can Cry Can Scream.

You can cry, you can scream but

you'll never be seen or heard...

If those tears and voice is meaningful.

When you love someone but you're scared

you do foolish things because you don't

want to get hurt.

Sometimes you just don't realize,

closest is what you really need.

Loving someone is a great feeling but being

loved back is even greater.

When you find that person who completes you

play your cards smart and

never let go.

Wanting To Run.

When there's a time of disagreement...

Your heart fights with itself to end the battle.

Only cause the love for one another is there,

with all its love.

There maybe times when you'll want to walk away

from situation like this

but...

because of the love, you are like a baby,

who hasn't start walking.

Now you crawl but you only get so far.

The question is how far...

is it far enough to start over

or

is it not enough to take you away.

Always Wanted.

The man you always wanted.

You open your front door to find that perfect man.

Your heart falls and he catches it.

Trouble times are always there throughout

But...

with the love for one another,

trouble times are blowed away like...

sand on the beach.

And ...

Love is always there to hold on to.

Fix It.

Why try to fix...

Fix things that can't be fix.

Try to grow a relationship...

Grow a relationship into joy

but

whatever you do you always seem to fail.

You may ask yourself why care several times

But...

You can't stop!

When you love someone,

for you to stop...

that's the hardest thing.

So now what do you do?

That's the question.

Voices.

Only voices of argue.

Voices of misunderstanding

Voices of no care

Voices of no understanding

No more lovemaking

No more laughter's

No more hand-in-hand walks

No more passionate kisses

No more love messages on the phone

What more does one need to take

how much heartache can one heart take.

It always seems as the heart is always

willing to try.

Even ... if ...It causes it pain.

Wouldn't let go.

Inner Most.

All my innermost fantasies shared with you.

After that I knew it was going to be

you and me.

No one would ever know us the way

we know us.

Even if you and me are only an image.

It would be the greatest image

to see.

Trying To Forget.

Trying to forget moments of the

un-imaginable moments.

Moments of so much inner thoughts

that just kept your mind traveling to height of the unknown.

Moments when your inner thoughts

travel into your dreams.

Having you wake up in a warm heated fire

and not sure you could ever get out.

Moments of you screaming in your sleep

no more... no more...

Dreams of moments that have you fighting with your mind.

A trouble mind ... troubles everything.

When trying to forget...comes moments,

come dreams, comes trouble mind,

comes good but sometimes bad.

BREAK UP

Sometimes love is letting go. Don't want to smile anymore...why should you when it hurts inside.

Full Of Surprise.

Life is full of surprise.

One day at a time, at a minute, at a second

What do you think happens?

Do you hear laughter?

Or

Do you hear tears of sorrow?

Whatever you hear you know that in one

way or the other.

Someone is always there.

Always there to hear when you call, the question is,

are they always going to keep running to you?

You always know when you got something real because if

you

can overcome bad times then it shows there's

a real strong feeling.

With this special person, it's so hard when

you love someone.

And at one point in time you get this feeling that

it almost ended.

The question is what are you suppose to do now?

Do you roll over and cry?

Or

Do you just let it be?

Did What Was Done.

Your heart maybe hurting but maybe...

You should have thought about that before doing what was

done.

Few years later, you started to wonder why the

relationship isn't the way it was before

did you ever stop to think...

maybe because of those years back when you

did what was done.

Now all you can do is lie in bed crying, wondering...

How to fix the broken pieces.

You may try glue, but that only un-sticks.

The love for this person, is going to cause

you the tears at night.

Cause this love one is hurting and that's not what you

wanted.

You messed up something good

You brought nothing but heartache to yourself!

What does one do now?

Future is none, none of the best.

5 a.m.

5 o'clock in the morning and I haven't slept yet

waiting for...for what I'm not even sure but

my body is unhappy and is waiting for

something ... something.

I'm starting to feel like I don't even

understand myself so how is another going to understand

me.

One should be beside of me,...love me.

But not rolling in at 5 am and waking me up

to work on his schedule.

Cause that just shows that I, his wife,

is the last on his list.

Maybe...this late night is for me but what

good is it going to be when

one is so unhappy.

even know.

How Do You Stay?

How do you stay

in love with someone who doesn't attend to you?

How do you find the words to tell him your heart is in pain

cause of the life style he's in.

How much do you have to take before he can

truly see what it is doing to you.

Love him...

Is the only thing I have left but how do you do that

when you can't even receive it back.

But when you receive you always

seem to be last on his list.

Not a buyer, you aren't on the head of the list.

I'm tired...tired

Completely tired, even

tired to cry, to let out the pain.

Exact Special.

All you want is to be held to be loved...

To be touch in the most sexual way you could think of.

You're now tired of going to bed alone...

You need to be felt up and down...

You don't just want to hear the words "I love you"

You want to feel it.

You just want someone who can make you feel that

exact special.

Making a woman feel exact special is the key

to all her happiest.

Love is a hard thing but it shouldn't be...

But when one always know you're always going to be

there...

he now takes his time.

His time has now ran out.!

Pain - Wonderful.

Pain is a wonderful thing...

It may not be the best feeling but

the end is always better than the beginning.

Pain is something that we learn from, never take pain to put

yourself to a lower level in your life.

Take pain and better yourself to the fullest that the pain

can give.

Pain is beautiful!!!

Thanking the people who hurt you is the first step to

changing the hurt of pain into laughter of pain.

Pain that no longer feels like pain.

Pain on a whole different level...where pain now feels like

getting

a dozen roses from someone special.

Pain...Beautiful...Thankful for pain.

Letting Go.

How do you let go of something that's

not even there?

How do you stop your emotions from feeling a certain way.

A second object that's, all you

really are.

Second on every single list made.

But no one ever wants to feel second.

So you read that letter that made it seem as you were

#ONE

But actions...

Say more than words on a piece of paper.

Heartfelt Feelings.

What is one do when the love for one...

Starts to feel like it's being destroy.

How does one overlook all the hurtful things said in argue

so they can fix everything.

Can this be fixed...the way it needs to be fix.

Or...

Has damage already been done to the fullest.

Everything should be fixable but when fix is it going

to be the same.

Or...

Is it a new world...then the next question is do I want a new

world?

No! I want exactly what I had when we first held hands.

Things feel so different.

Sleeping Mind.

Your mind working overtime...

Sleeping but solutions and decisions are being placed in

the mind.

We're at a point now where two separate directions

are our only answers.

But...

Just like human's we know what has to be done, we're just

scared.

Scared of something new when we're comfortable with old.

But when old no longer look promising.

You have to let go.

A person at each end of the rope,

tug 'n 'war, someone has to cut the middle...Or...

Someone just had to save the rope from breaking

and just let go.

How You Going To Act...

Now you ask...

How I'm going to act like that?

Can I ask...

How you going to put your hands on me?

Then you say you're sorry and believe that should fix the

wrong.

Now I walk out the door.

And...

You finally realized I expected my wrongs.

And you now have to realize your wrongs.

The only way I could open your eyes was by leaving.

Leaving and being on my own.

It's Sad.

It's sad when you had something so good and now it's all

ended.

Cause you are tired...

Tired of being sad, tired of crying.

So, something that was to be magical

is now over.

Friendship!

Sadly that's all that remains.

CHANGES

What's new under the sun? Changes can be good as well as bad. Just cause it hurts it doesn't mean it's not right.

Close Your Eyes & Dream.

Close your eyes and dream.

What do you see?

Do you see happiness or do you see sadness.

Is there someone who is ready to give

all he got.

Is this the person that you can laugh in front of...

You can cry in front of...

You can just totally be yourself in front of...

Open now...

Then close again.

The question now is...

"is that same person there?"

Lost.

Have your heart ever felt so lost that you almost though it

would be nearly impossible.

Loving a man to the fullest is something of the beyond.

You always tell yourself something can be changed...

So you can feel completely happy with your choice.

But...

Something's just don't change

Now, what do you do?

You start looking at all the positive things.

Now you say to yourself that you can live without those

un-changeable things.

But...

The real questions is can you truly live

without?

A Change.

Have you ever felt forgotten...

At least forgotten for a day or part of a day.

One day it's constant touching feeling... eye contact.

But...in a split second of going to bed and waking up

there's no more touching, feeling not even eye contact.

Now you lie in bed asking yourself...

Is it something I did or didn't do?

Loving someone is the craziest feeling,

so many emotions run wild.

All you can think is hopefully it's not me.

You are also thinking, why couldn't he just come and

let you know what the deal is so you can

sleep somewhat comfortably.

Have you ever cried so much, deeply inside...cause it hurts

so much

the tears can't even find their way out so they just cry within.

Have you ever hurt so much for things that shouldn't even

hurt you...

But emotions the uncontrollable, that is faith.

Haven't you ever try to change things back but

you just don't know how...

so you make yourself available hoping that he would

make the turn.

But no turn...

Now you are crying inside again.

Tears of a change.

Unknown Changes.

Life changes everyday...

Sometimes the changes are good and sometimes the

changes are bad.

All you can do is keep an open mind of the changes.

Sometimes changes you have no control over but you truly

wish that these things wouldn't change.

You are wanting to turn back time, not even knowing

what change is coming.

One day can change your life forever.

It's like going to the interview for that job you always

wanted.

And whatever the results... good or bad

it's going to change your life.

Bad: you always wonder why you didn't get it or what you

could have done differently.

Good : new plans for your future. A new person all

together.

One day can change everything.

Have you ever wanted to say yes so bad.

But...you knew saying no or nothing was the rightful thing.

Something where your whole life depended on it.

Something where if you said yes your life could be great

And...

If you said no...your life would be good but for some reason

it wouldn't be as good as if you said yes.

Life changing with no notice changing with difficult decision.

Every decision comes with emotions,

cause a decision should come from the heart.

Life isn't meant to be easy!

The Doors.

I feel like doors are closing on me but

doors of fantasy are opening every second.

I feel like I'm living a dream life

But...

Sometimes I feel like I'm living a nightmare.

I feel like there's one door in my life that I have

opened and walked halfway in...

then paused.

Cause...I'm scared of falling too deep.

It's dark... but I see this light but scared to find out

who's holding on the other end.

Why?...I just don't know.

Future.

How does one make life decisions...

When not sure of what the future holds.

Life is a gamble

But...

It is taught to us that we shouldn't gamble.

So how is one to make decision for their lives

Maybe...just maybe...

I'm suppose to just go with the flow.

How does this work?

Emotion.

One minute your whole world can change...

Cause of emotions.

So uncontrollable...

If something is meant ... it will find it's way.

Maybe it will take a minute

Maybe it will take a hour

Maybe it will take a day

Maybe it will take a month or

Maybe it will take a year.

It's not time

It's event.

Are your emotions always right...

Cause emotions comes from the heart...

Shouldn't it be right?

Dead End.

Crying until you can't cry anymore.

Caring until you can't care anymore.

Loving and continue loving...

Mix emotions...so uncontrollable the end of the road.

When you come to a dead end you always seem to want to

go straight

But...

It's decision time...

Left or right?

Inner Self- Confusion.

Have you ever found out things about yourself...

That just doesn't seem right.

You are starting to see a need for change but not sure...

Cause one man seems to think a certain way of you.

Your innermost feelings are being juggled around in a

glass...

Now you are trying to fix them in there

rightful place.

Words of the confused...

Words of the...need of help crying out.

Words of the heart & soul.

Words of questions that seems to be answer but just...

You know!!!

Have you ever had your heart give you

two answers to a question and now...

you just don't know which road would be better...

or...

maybe you know the better road, you are just scared

of crossing the river by yourself.

To control fear you have to believe in yourself.

You need to try.

Try and believe

Confuse...not! you need to tell yourself.

Sunny Days. vs. Rainy Days

I'm tired...so tired of the tears of those rainy days.

It seem like it rain so much tears that now I'm in a flood...

No way out.

I'm tired... so tired!

I'm ready and deserve sunny days

Day of laughter, smiles and all little things.

I'm ready for those warm moments.

Ready for true affection...

Affection of understanding the emotions.

Every feelings counts...understanding.

People are always around

Some are there for good causes

and

some are there for the complete opposite.

Some are there to love you

and

some are there to hate you.

Causing you pain and heartache taking you happiest and

destroying it.

Some people just can't accept the fact that things have

changed.

But the question is... do they have a choice.

Sometimes things change and

that's just the way it has to be.

CRIES

For not knowing the pain you couldn't know the world blessings. Tears the water of blessings. (It may hurt)

Hope.

Hope for better life...

Hope for the oppression to stop...

Hope for love and comfort...

Why is no one hearing my cries for hope?

Why is no one hearing my prayers for hope?

Someone please take away these tears,

someone please hear my prays.

Someone!

Anyone!

Please!

Beyond The Beyond.

I want life beyond the beyond.

I want life for what it truly should be...

For the better of the people regardless of color, religion,

age and sex.

The beyond of the beyond is comfort.

No! the humanize world would never be comfortable

cause the human beings are selfish and want power.

Power for what?

We ask, cause we are all equal in Gods eyes no matter

what one thinks they have over another.

There is only one power

our father.

Some nights I just want to cry...

Cry for what I'm not even sure anymore.

Some days can start up so good, having so much fun.

But...

Something as simple as a mood change

can now make the clouds cry...

cry out to understand.

All you want is to love, you just want to know what's wrong.

But...

For some reason you are now tongue tie and

can't find the words to ask if it was something

said or done.

Take Away The Pain.

How do you take away the pain?

How do you stay where you just don't feel comfortable.

Comfortable in the sense that your heart seems as if it's

constantly hurting.

Hurting in the sense that, what you want, seems so far away

but actually beside you...

but cause of situations and emotions...

you would reach out but it's just not enough.

As human's we don't know nor understand how to let go, we

always seem to put ourselves through so much to have, what

sometimes is just not there.

If someone knows the answer to my question.

Please answer for me

Please tell me.

Cries Away

I hear the cries

I understand the cries

But I no longer want the cries.

I feel a need to run...run away.

A need to be beyond my own opening of newer doors

with newer life experiences.

Only 20yrs, haven't seen the world yet haven't learn

enough...

Tired of all the tears, tears from my eyes

tears from love ones eyes

tears from all over the world.

Tell Someone.

How do you tell someone you care but things have change.

Beside...

Saying it actually how I just said it.

How do you tell someone situations just aren't the same.

Beside...

Saying it actually how I just said it.

How do you tell someone they are pushing you away slowly

without even knowing it.

Beside...

Saying it actually how I just said it.

How do you tell someone to stop crying over you...

cause you know your not worth it.

Beside...

Saying it actually how I just said it.

How do you tell someone...

Emotion good or bad at times

Loving one with future plans but out of no where

emotions show you another door.

With no intentions to hurt the other person you open and

walk in.

To find yourself with mix feelings.

So you let go of yourself with no control.

Hoping for what you're not sure.

Tables have turn and all the hurt and pain is on you.

No more you can truly say to fix it.

You can only sit back and wait for your turn of

disappointment.

You want to say your sorry and it wasn't your intentions

to hurt anyone put the pain of that person would always

overlook the fact that it wasn't intended to hurt them.

Cry To God.

I have done some bad things in life but this feels the worst.

I was just moving with what I felt inside...

I thought that was always the right way.

On my way I wasn't thinking of others...

in no way was I intentional trying to hurt anyone.

But...

At the same time I just couldn't hide what I felt inside...I was

weak.

Emotional weak!

Now cause of the hurt I have cause people.

I'm physically hurt and I fear there is no care.

I'm the type that lets emotions

run with me.

My feelings have destroy others and for that

I'm truly sorry!

Have you ever thought so hard that you make yourself

feint...

You're walking and feel as if nothing is below you.

Thinking of all the pain you cause people...now you are

physically and emotionally destroyed inside.

You now don't even know how to hold yourself together.

You cry when someone shows you love and you just listen

when someone cusses you.

Have you ever thought so hard that your heart just seems

as if it's getting smaller and smaller by the minute...

so now you think how long for you to live.

Have you ever though so hard and wondered if there

was anything truly worth living for.

Then I think...

God gave me this life...even with all my wrongs and all I can

do is

try and make it right.

In God's eye

I truly hope that I can make it right...take away the pain if it

means

letting me have nothing at all.

My Sunshine.

It's me, and you in this together

You maybe missing me

You are ok, it may look more than it really is.

But...

We are friends for life.

I'm sorry...

It was just getting hard to see,

hard to see what was

needed.

I'm Sorry.

I'm sorry...

But this is what I wanted maybe...

I'm being selfish but sometimes I guess you do have to

think about yourself.

Maybe...just maybe...

You'll be able to forgive me.

It's just the way it has to be for me at least.

I'm sorry!

You use to love a man to the point of no return.

Then somewhere along the way, love just turned into care!

Why?

I can't tell you

How?

I'm just not sure.

A man's life is being destroy now...

How do you just turn back to ease his pain.

When, what was there before isn't there any more.

But...

Still so hard cause your heart still cares.

Now...you look at yourself in the mirror with not much to say

for yourself

Seeing...

That's some thing you are just not.

I'm sorry doesn't seem to ease the pain.

But...

That's truly how I feel...

What do I do now?

Now I sit here...

4 o'clock in the morning looking at my past life.

All I have is tears of no understanding

What Went Wrong?

Did I miss a lesson to be learn?

Or...

Is my life, what it is

20yrs with so many ups and downs.

Wondering when time will grow in my favor.

What Went Wrong?

No one to answer my questions but... myself

I just don't know

What Went Wrong?

Replacements.

When you are sad or upset

you always try to replace that

with something that may take away the pain.

Sometimes you may just try to get

the hurt out by screaming.

Breaking things Slamming doors.

Sometimes you may even try just crying it all out...

Which could take all night.

Sometimes you may eat or drink the pain away.

Then there are times when you would just put on

the radio to the jazz station.

Something to ease the soul

And...

If you are anything like me...when it really hurts.

You write the pain away.

FROM THE SOUL

Nothing more true than the soul.

Struggles.

Why does one struggles so much?

How does one get themselves into things, when payback is

right around?

How does one who was so clean become so dirty?

How does one fix the mess...wash away all the negative and

start life over with all positive attitude and vibe?

Right roads before wrong roads...

Correction, the sign to better future and life.

Being thankful for what is actually given to you and

not things you thought you could steal.

Thankfulness!

Is a wonderful thing.

Respect.

I have seen respect to a whole other level.

A level of realizing that you can't have

everything you want in life

but you still...

Open your eyes to the unknown.

Just do things with a good heart

and everything will always seem right

but better yet it will be

right.

Your Heart.

Your heart

feel something of the unknown.

But...

Your heart wants to know the unknown.

So it looks for some way to know

without bring attention of others.

You know what I mean...?

Open.

Open your mind, open your eyes and open your heart.

And let

your heart take you places you never thought you could go.

For the unknown is meant to be known.

And the only way you can know

the unknown is by letting your heart open to the

un-open-able.

Where nothing is a secret.

Travel Affection.

Letting your heart travel...

Travel...to higher levels

Levels of the unknown...the unknown of which

you'll like to find out.

No one like, not knowing something.

Even if very small.

Action thought is the hardest things not to think of.

You always want to know the feelings...

the way you will feel upon the action being done.

It is like thinking of the way it would feel to be in a burning

building.

Does it hurt?...and how much?

Just like something good...does it feel really good?

And how good, is going through your mind.

AFFECTION!

No Reason.

Have your mind been so trouble with so many things

that you no longer know what

you think about.

You no longer know why you are in a bad mood.

It just seems right at that point.

You could start off your day wonderful...

Then come home and take a nap...

To wake-up in bad mood of

no known reason.

Unforgettable.

How do you try and forget moments?

When trying is thinking about the moment.

You have to think

of the moment

to forget the moment.

Maybe remembering

is needed.

I'm Trying.

I'm trying to understand...

Understand these humans for who they are.

Everyone is different.

Some are sweet and some are not.

Humans always find someway to play with your emotions.

I'm trying to understand...

Understand these humans.

I just can't find the door of understanding.

You just share your innermost feelings...just to feel step on.

Maybe you are over reacting but maybe not.

Understanding humans are the hardest thing cause

there's too much emotions involved.

Why don't we ever talk to each other when

something is on our mind...

just like I'm doing pen and paper is

my solution for hurt and argues.

Some solutions for these humans are drinking, smoking,

messing around, breaking things, suicide .

What has these humans done to

mother-earth.

Including me.

Words Of...

Have you ever received something from someone?

That made you feel so special words of which ran

chills through your body.

Words of which made you think of this person

constantly.

But as soon as these words were read everything change

when it came to actions.

Words are so easy to write but to actually

say it and mean it....

Different topic!

Why- O- Why.

Why does life have to be so crazy?

Why does everything happen the way it does?

Why does life seem so unfair at times?

Why is it that everything you do or say is something

you have to live with everyday?

Why is a lie, a lie and the truth, is the truth?

Why-o-why?

I'm Tired.

I'm tired of fighting with myself

inside my innermost feelings are feeling like they are

swimming around in a jar

with no way out.

I'm tired of trying to make decisions,

especially when it's a decision of so much emotions.

One say you must control your emotions...and...

don't let it control you.

How?

When emotions are what makes you the person you are.

I'm tired of seeing my life as my past experiences.

I'm trying to move forward but something is always in my

pathway.

I'm tired of sitting up late at nights writing about

my pains and sorrows.

I'm tired of crying the tears of pain...

I believe I don't have anymore of those tears.

Have you ever had something happen that you didn't want

and you try to control your emotions,

so you don't make the situation worst.

But...

The question now, is , were you able to control the

emotions?

Answer: no!

Why?

Answer: unexplainable.

I'm tired.

Every time you try to get some sleep it

just doesn't seem to work.

You keep yourself busy throughout the day..., which

leaves...

emotions.

Emotions to deal with at nights.

So what do you do?...so you can get some rest.

You may take a long hot shower

You may read something

You may write like I do...get all your thoughts on paper.

But...

The truth you never get all your thoughts on paper

cause some things are too personal to your heart...no words

can explain.

So another sleepless night.

Unashamed.

Unashamed of the life I live.

Unashamed of the love I have chose.

I don't think I would be where I am today if not for my

mistake.

Mistakes of no regrets.

To be part of my life you need to see

I'm unashamed.

No regrets cause it's a learning experience...

Only something to make me

stronger.

Closing Eyes.

I'm closing my eyes on everything

negative in this world.

And...

Opening my eyes to the more positive things.

Hoping that with me looking forward instead of back,

things will just fall into place.

Not making things happen but letting it happen

by nature.

Everything You Wanted.

Now you have everything you wanted.

The life that is comfortable, loving and so relaxed.

You should be happy!

Happy you are but at the same time sad and confused.

Why?

The way your joy came into your life was wonderful.

But...

Destroy close ones to you, damages that just can't be

forgotten...

That just can't be changed.

All I want is a man who loves to spend time with me.

All I want is a man who can understand me.

I want a man who can say he truly enjoy being with me.

A man who knows how to make me laugh.

A man who can always put a smile on my face

even when I'm having a bad day.

A man who say something and actually does that.

All I want is honesty, love,

affection and respect.

Bold.

Would I be bold to say I want you home now.

Would I be bold to say...

I want you to hold me and not let go.

Would I be bold to say...

I want you to kiss me with no limits.

Would I be bold to say...

when I need you I want you to be by my side.

A woman needs a man she can call her best friend.

A woman needs a man that would talk

with his woman when something

ain't right.

A woman needs a man that can open her eyes

to understanding each other.

Every woman definitely needs a man that can understand

her to the extent of any situation, would always be a mild

stone and not a bomb.

A man that gives as much as he takes.

A man that makes you feel like the queen you are.

A man that can stand beside you as a king and not just a

man.

A man that knows a woman should have some

independence...

he would never make it that you have to

always depend on him.

A man that would do things together.

A man that would help you with bringing your qualities to

the highest.

And a man (king) that wouldn't be so manly

about you doing the same for him.

Together it's wisdom and strength.

Precious.

Have you ever thought about the beauty of marriage ?

The beauty of lovemaking!

Think about the hugs and kisses

you get when you come home from a hard day at work.

The time of the little ones running around

your wonderful household of a family.

It's precious and something

to cherish.

Alive.

Alive...

Have you ever felt so alive

that even the most tired day wasn't going to bring you down.

Not alive in the sense of energy

But...

Alive in the sense of mind & spirit.

Happiness overcoming everything.

May have assignments to finish

Maybe tired of work

But...for some reason you are still happy.

May have been the craziest day of your life but...still happy.

No explanation!

You want to ask yourself why, but...

at the same time this happiest has been away for a while.

So you chose not to answer that question now.

Maybe later.

Cherish all the happy moments you get.

Remember.

Remember the time when Christmas was about Christ and

family.

Now Christmas is about how much gifts you're going to get

this year.

Remember the first step of boyfriend and girlfriend, where

the guy would do anything to impress you.

Now you realize after a year that was all an act.

Remember the love growing within a family.

Now you don't even know who to trust or depend on.

Remember when every child was taught to pray at nights and

mornings.

Now they are cussing and killing at the age 10.

Remember when children were showing total respect to

parents.

Now children are calling their parents by their first name and

cussing at them...children taking their own road.

Everyone trying to do things by themselves and

not with our father at heart.

Free Education.

People waste their time and money on this thing call school...

When others can't even feed themselves, far less feed their

family.

If school is so important then it should be free...

But ...no! cause they know everyone would be in school

educating themselves.

But one thing they forgot is that you don't need

school(building) to educate yourself

Education is free!

School is not!

In the end this is all about lessons and learning from them, so you can better your life. I'm unashamed of the life I have lived, and grateful for the mistakes made, cause it made me who I am today.

I thank my queen for giving birth to me.... and helping me see life is a world of lessons. This is something that has always been within me, just never thought my thoughts would become a book. A special thanks to a.k.a Monteezy who made me realize that this passion, could be so much more. I also give thanks to my ex-boyfriend a.k.a Natural, who was a big inspiration to my poems, years of experiences together.

I'm thankful for every happy moment but I'm even more thankful for the painful, heartfelt moments, the moments that makes me a stronger woman. Always remember once you learn from your mistakes it's not a

regret.

Thank you to all, which has been a big part of my

life, families, friends, ex-relationships and my love one, with

all of you this book was possible.

Thank you!

ISBN 141201019-5

9 781412 010191